KW-552-005

Contents

Making a start

Learning to draw is about looking and seeing. Keep practising, use a sketchbook to make quick drawings and get to know your subject. Start by doodling and experimenting with shapes and movement. There are many ways to draw and this book shows only some of them. Visit art galleries, look at artists' drawings and see how friends draw, but above all, find your own way.

On average, a person's overall height is about 8 times the size of their head.

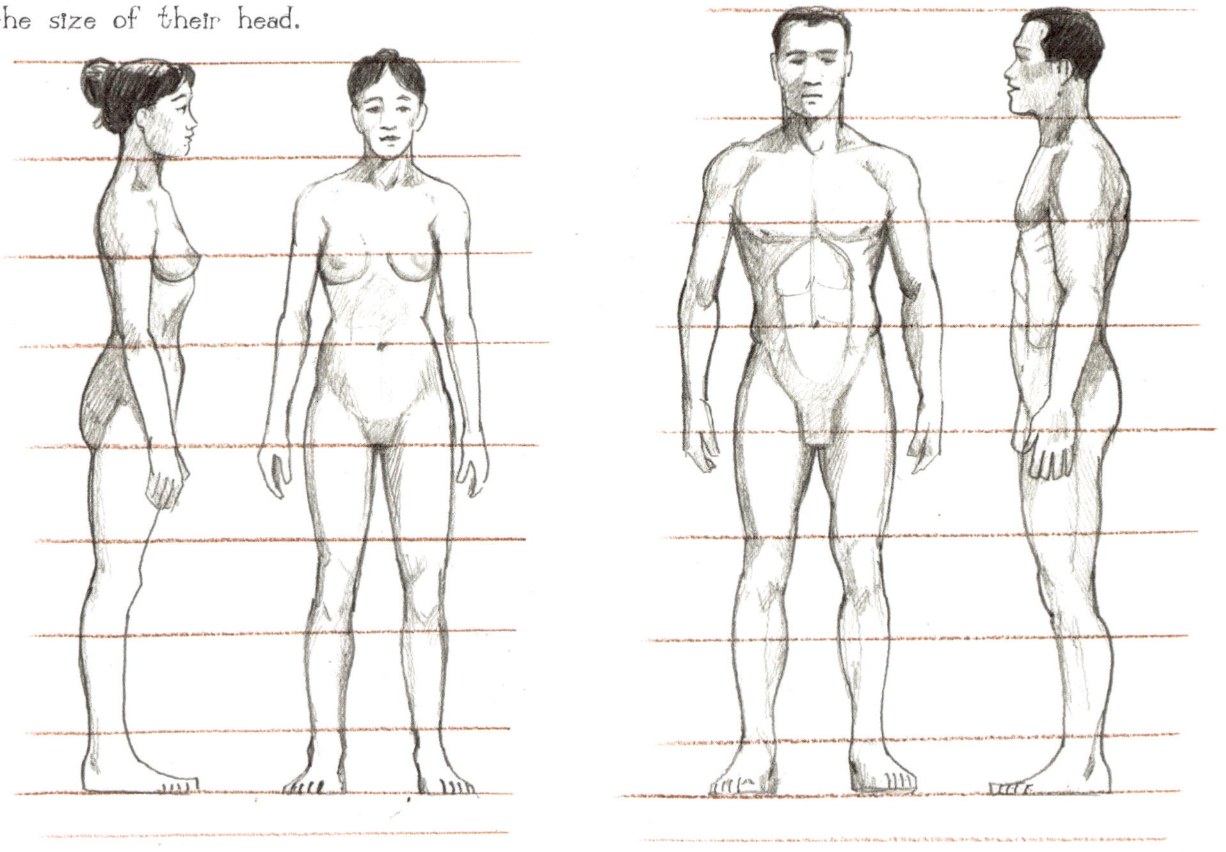

HOW … RAW™

DI … NG

4/10/19

BUN

Please renew or return items by the date shown on your receipt

www.hertfordshire.gov.uk/libraries

Renewals and enquiries: 0300 123 4049

Textphone for hearing or speech impaired users: 0300 123 4041

Hertfordshire

L32 11.16

Mark Bergin

BOOK HOUSE

528 983 34 8

Published in Great Britain in MMXVIII by
Book House, an imprint of
The Salariya Book Company Ltd
25 Marlborough Place, Brighton BN1 1UB
www.salariya.com

ISBN: 978-1-912006-30-4

SALARIYA
SCRIBO BOOK HOUSE SCRIBBLERS

© The Salariya Book Company Ltd MMXVIII
All rights reserved. No part of this publication may be reproduced, stored in or introduced into a retrieval system or transmitted in any form, or by any means (electronic, mechanical, photocopying, recording or otherwise) without the written permission of the publisher. Any person who does any unauthorised act in relation to this publication may be liable to criminal prosecution and civil claims for damages.

1 3 5 7 9 8 6 4 2

A CIP catalogue record for this book is available from the British Library.

Printed and bound in China.

This book is sold subject to the conditions that it shall not, by way of trade or otherwise, be lent, resold, hired out, or otherwise circulated without the publisher's prior consent in any form or binding or cover other than that in which it is published and without similar condition being imposed on the subsequent purchaser.

Author: Mark Bergin was born in Hastings in 1961. He studied at Eastbourne College of Art and has specialised in historical reconstructions as well as aviation and maritime subjects since 1983. He lives in Bexhill-on-Sea with his wife and three children.

Editor: Nick Pierce

Visit
www.salariya.com
for our online catalogue and
free fun stuff.

PAPER FROM SUSTAINABLE FORESTS

Ancient Roman statue in Vaison-la-Romaine, France

The Bather by Albert Toft, 1915
V&A Museum, London

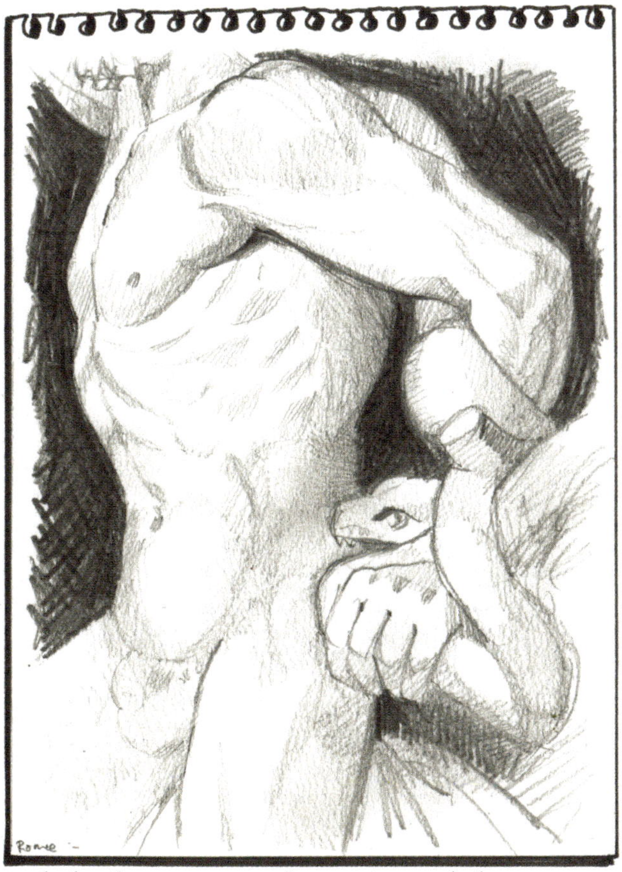

Detail of Laocoön and His Sons statue
Vatican Museum, Rome

Keep a sketchbook handy at all times. Make sketches of any artworks you see.

Drawing materials

Try using different types of drawing paper and materials. Experiment with charcoal, wax crayons and pastels. All pens, from felt-tips to ballpoints, will make interesting marks — or try drawing with pen and ink on wet paper.

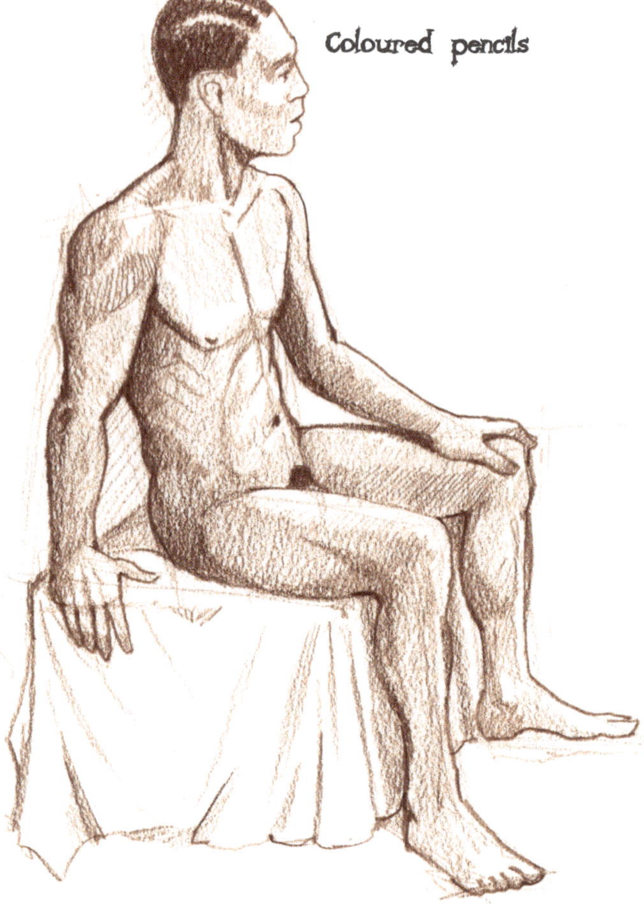

Coloured pencils

Coloured pencils come in a wide range of colours.

Ink pen

Lines drawn in **ink** cannot be erased, so keep your ink drawings sketchy and less rigid. Don't worry about mistakes, as these lines can be lost in the drawing as it develops.

Adding light and shade to a drawing with an ink pen can be tricky. Use solid ink for the very darkest areas and cross-hatching for less dark tones. Use hatching for midtones, and leave the white of the paper for the lightest areas.

Crosshatching is the use of straight lines that criss-cross each other. **Hatching** is when short parallel lines are used to create tone.

Conté crayon

Pencil drawings can include a vast amount of detail and tone. Try experimenting with different grades of pencil to get a good range of light and shade into your drawing.

Remember, the best equipment and materials will not necessarily make the best drawing – only practice will!

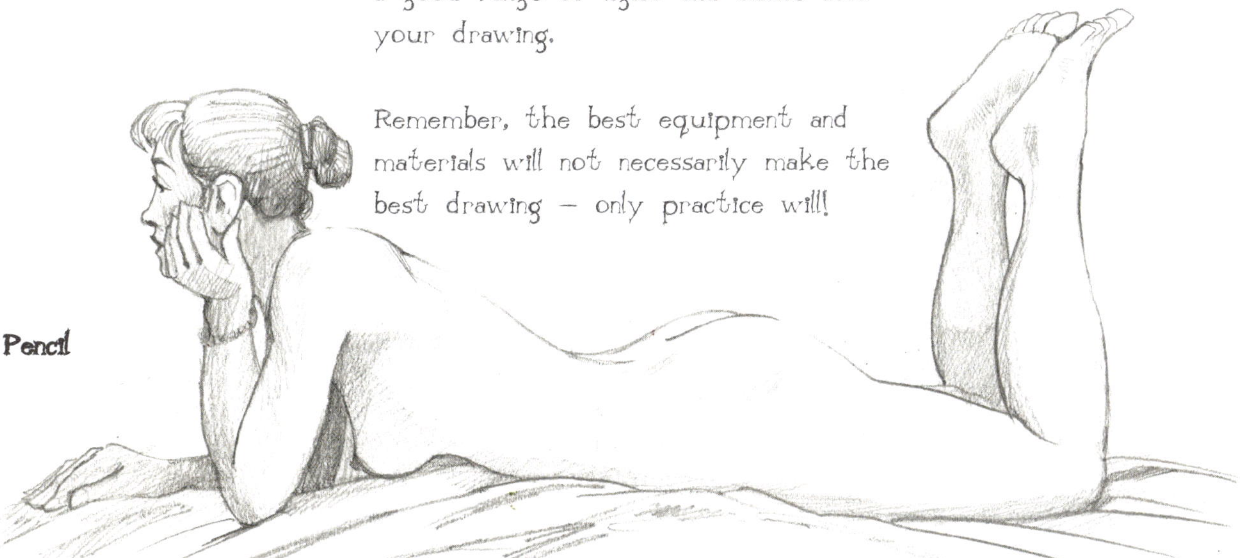

Pencil

Perspective

If you look at anything from different viewpoints, you will see that the part that is closest to you looks larger, and the part furthest away from you looks smaller. Drawing in perspective is a way of creating a feeling of space — of showing three dimensions on a flat surface.

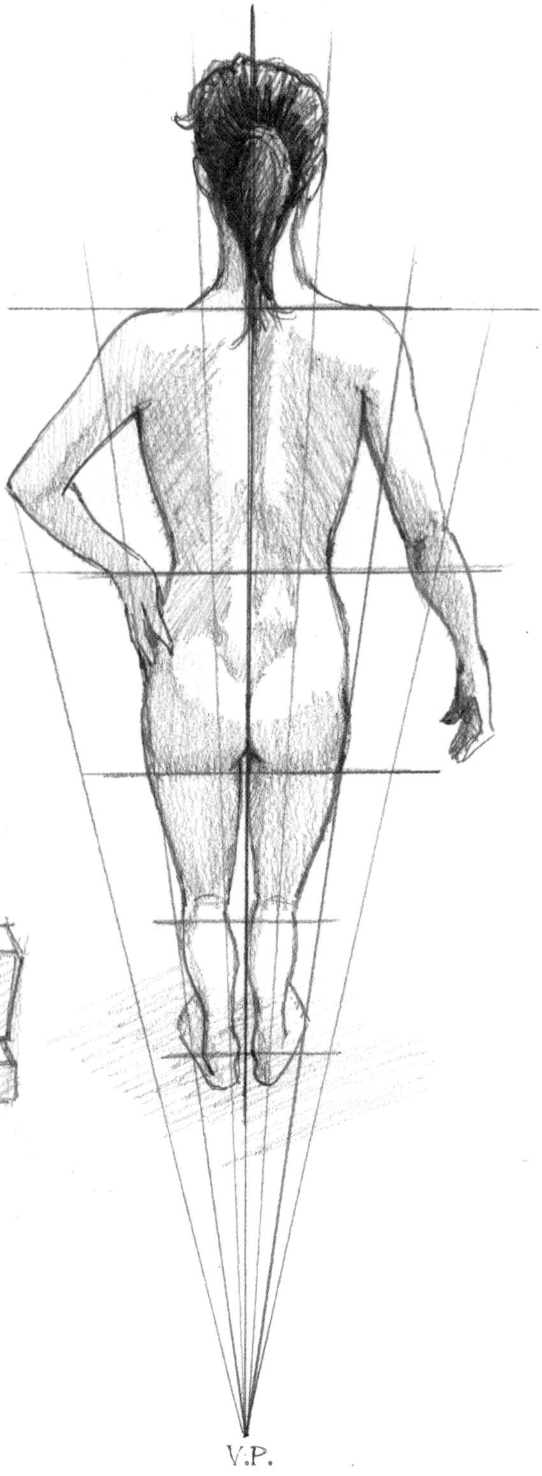

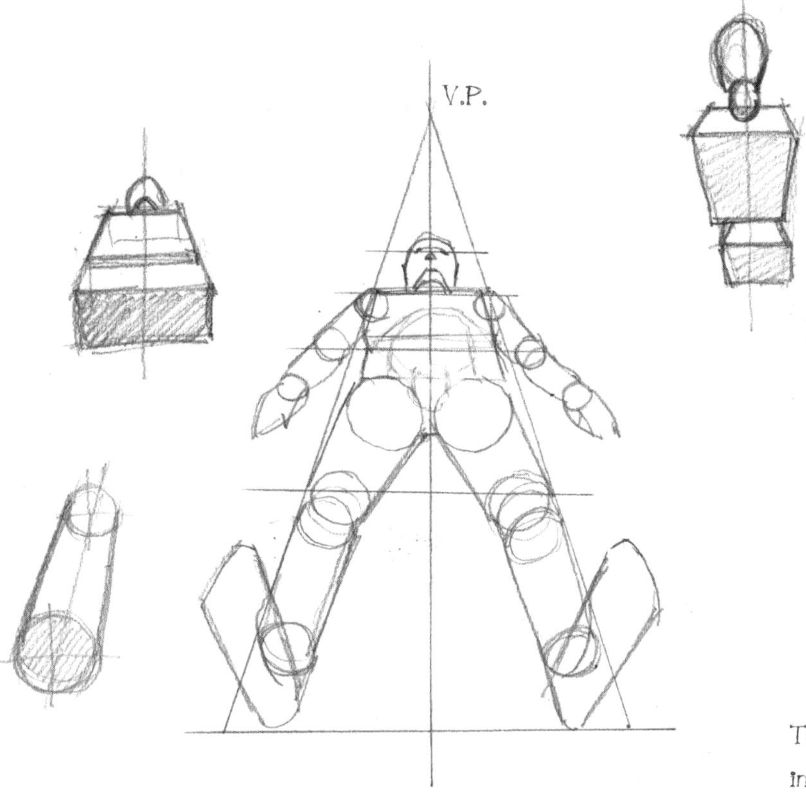

The vanishing point (V.P.) is the place in a perspective drawing where parallel lines appear to meet. The position of the vanishing point depends on the viewer's eye level.

Two-point perspective uses two vanishing points: one for lines running along the length of the subject, and one on the opposite side for lines running across the width of the subject.

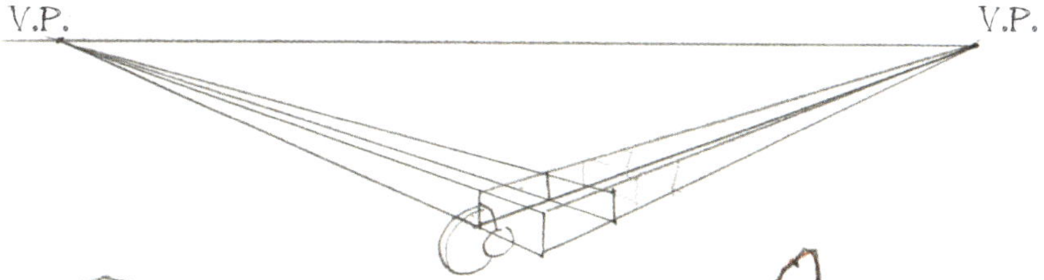

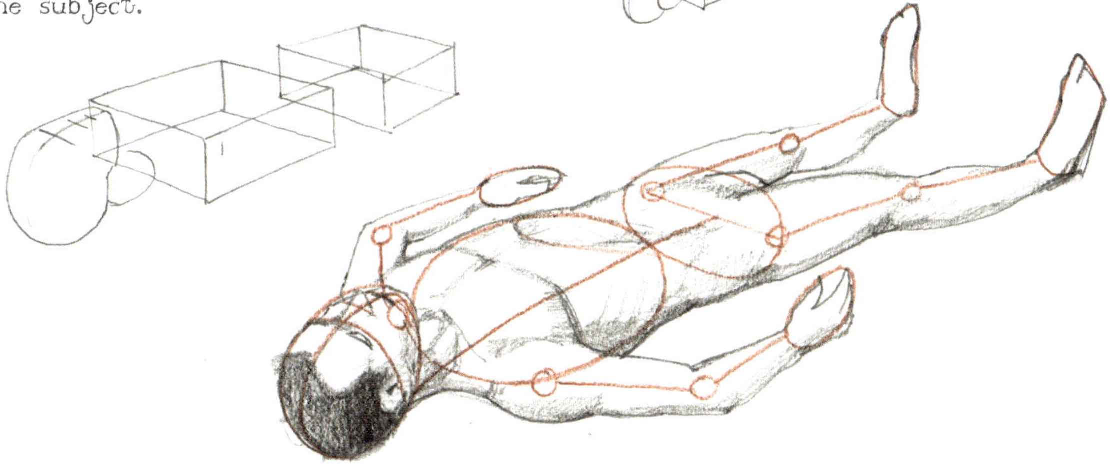

Three-point perspective drawings use three vanishing points. This method is good for drawing your subject from an angle.

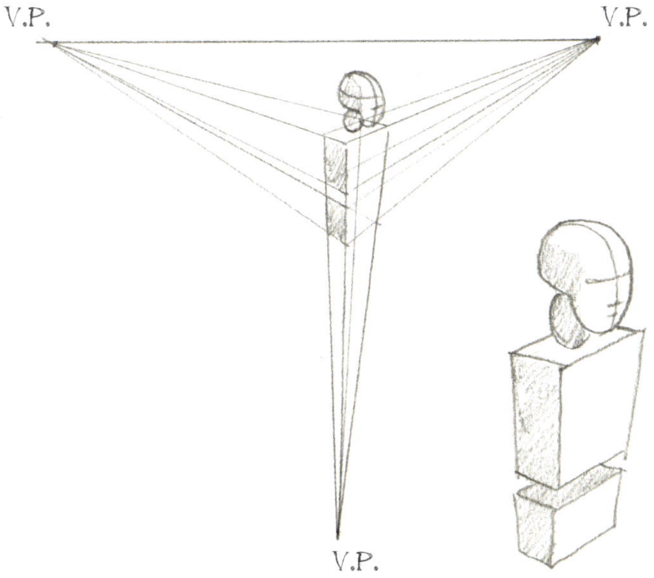

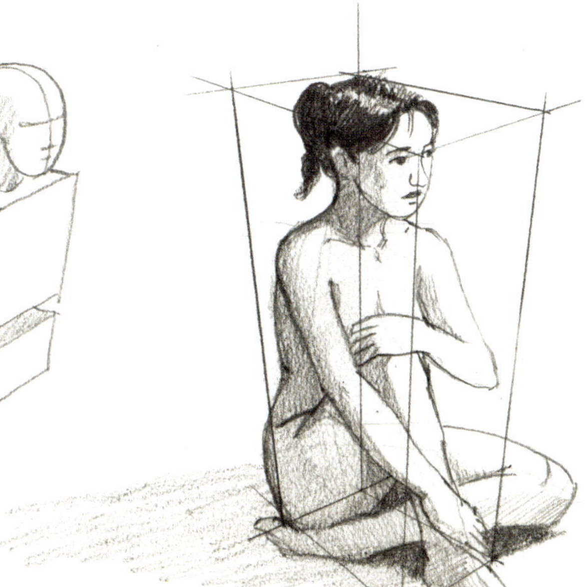

Anatomy & structure

Some understanding of the internal structure of the human body – the skeletal and muscle systems – will help you to draw more realistic nude studies that have solidity and life.

You can use an artist's mannequin figure to practise drawing people in different poses.

Use the skeletal structure to inform the outward form of your subject.

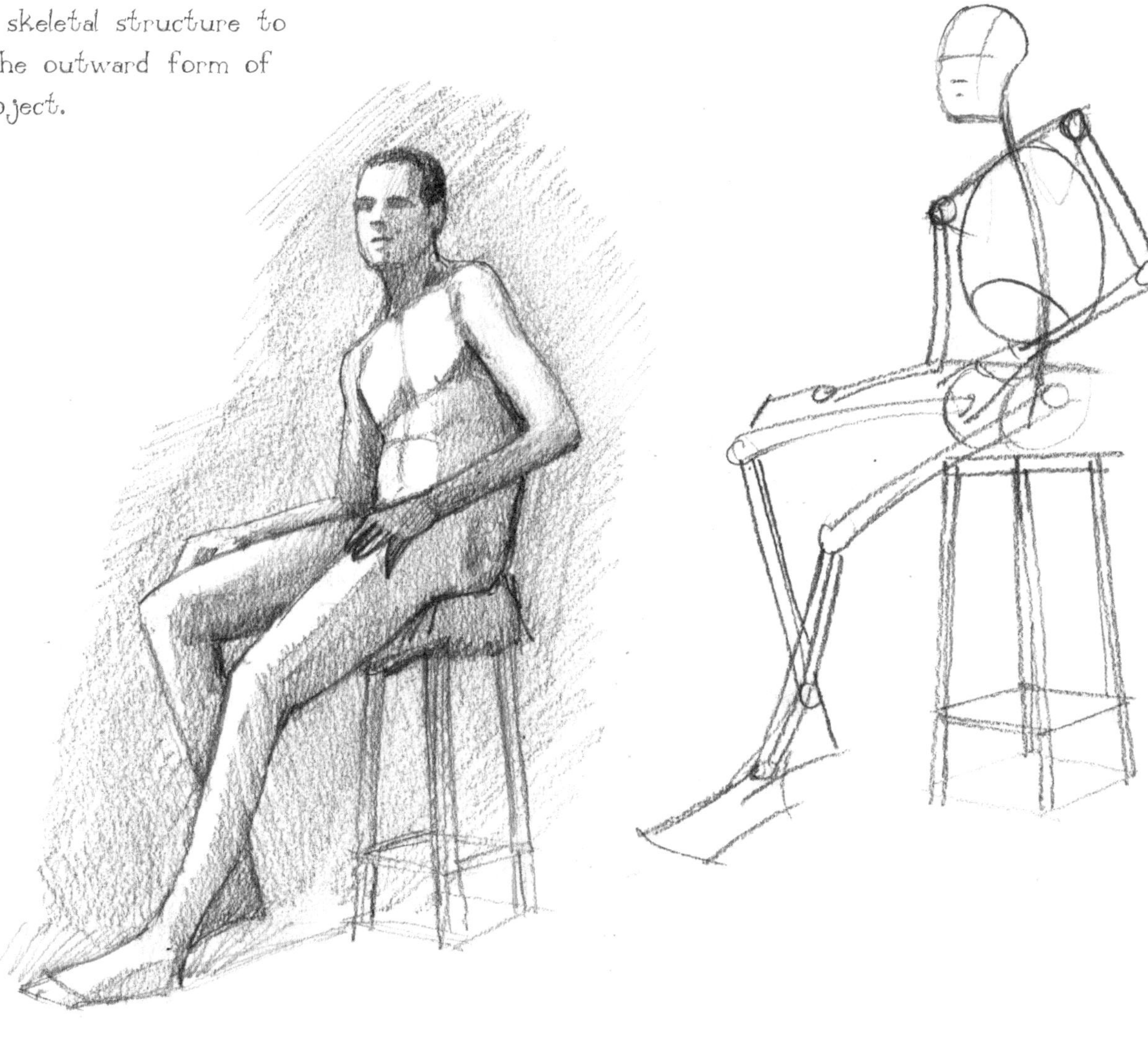

Ways of seeing a figure

Draw an outline of your subject to establish a better idea of its boundaries and the space surrounding it.

Use construction lines to position the limbs and joints of the figure so their positioning is anatomically correct.

Draw in the facial features and the hair. Add more definition to the shape of the figure's body.

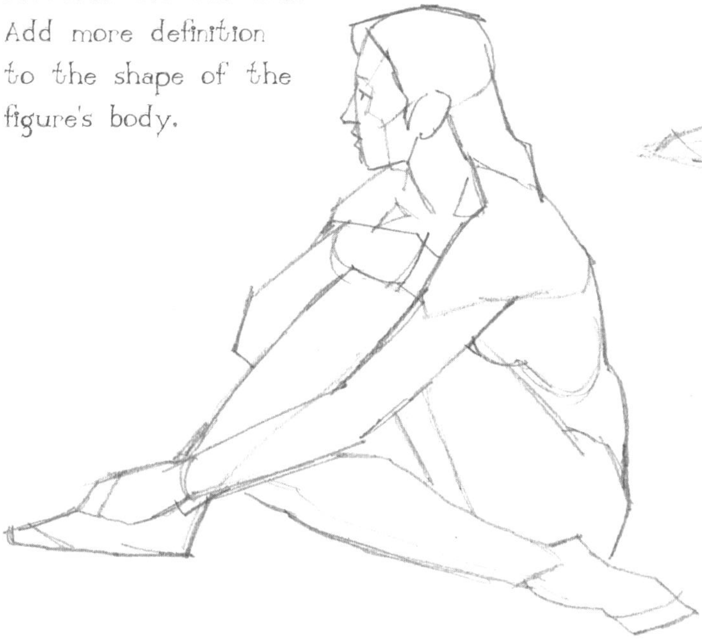

Add shading to highlight the different values of dark and light. Note how the direction of the light causes shadows to fall across the body. This makes the picture look more realistic.

Life drawing

Students attend life drawing classes to make observational drawings of a clothed or unclothed life model. Life drawing is fundamentally a way of training your eye and hand to work together to create an accurate and accomplished sketch within the time constraints of the model's poses.

Make sure your easel is at a comfortable angle.

It is best to have enough space to stand back and appraise your drawing.

Make sure you can see your drawing and the model at the same time to make direct comparisons as you work.

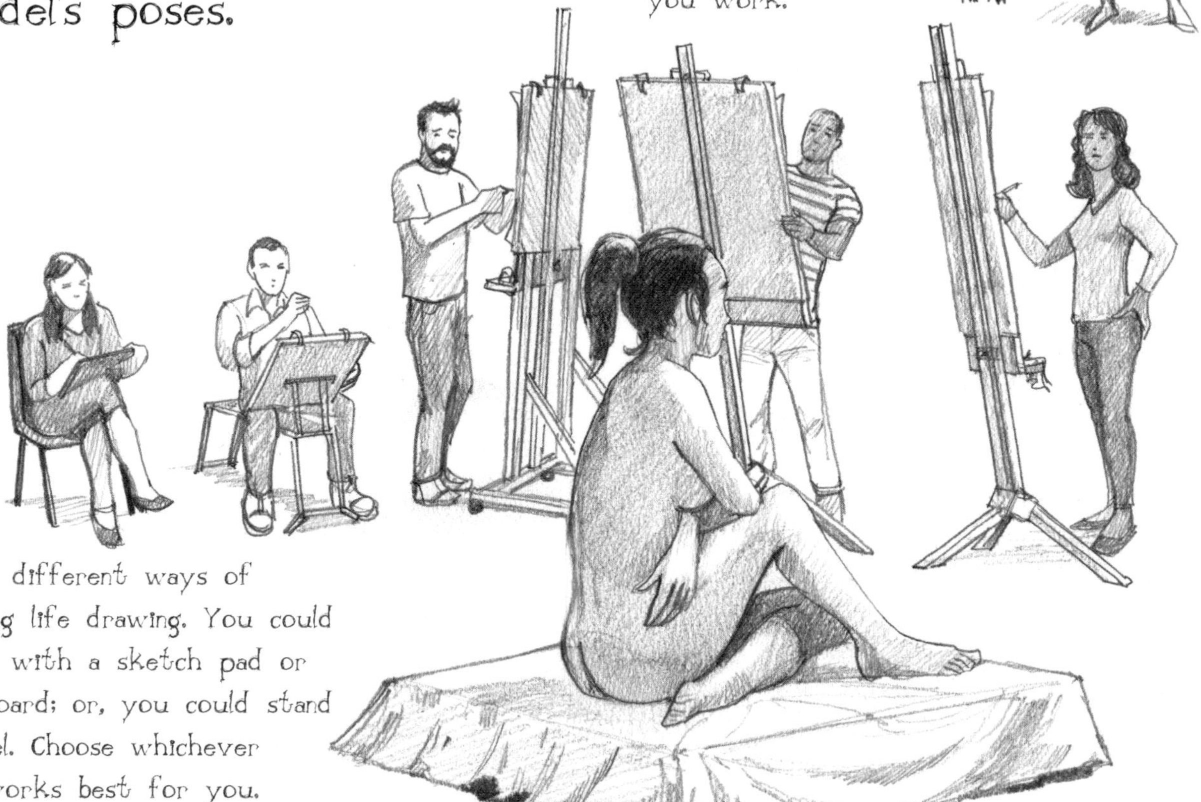

There are different ways of approaching life drawing. You could be seated with a sketch pad or drawing board; or, you could stand at an easel. Choose whichever method works best for you.

Study the model before you start drawing. Always take time to observe and familiarise yourself with the form, proportions and rhythms of each pose.

Do not concentrate on isolated details – try to see the drawing as a whole. Don't put off drawing areas you perceive as difficult, like hands or feet.

The more drawing you do the more you will enjoy the results. Practice really does make you look harder and draw better. Experiment to develop your own unique style.

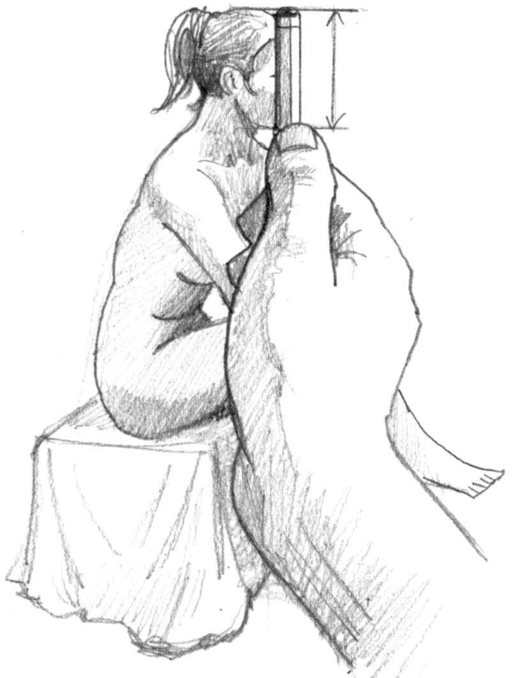

Don't be afraid to make mistakes. If a drawing goes wrong, just analyse it to understand why, and start again.

Quick poses

Making quick 1–3 minute sketches of nude figures in different poses is a good warm-up exercise. It requires quick observation and mark-making that launches you straight into 'drawing mode'. It hones your understanding of how a body changes shape as it moves.

Lunging

Bending over at the waist

Lunging, seen from back view

Crouching

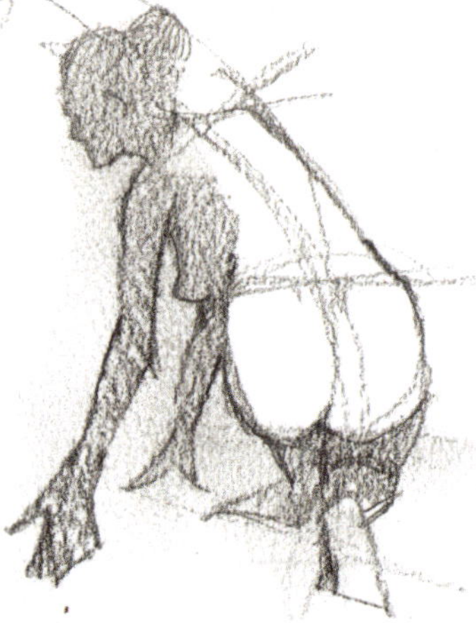

Crouching, seen from back view

Stretching

Lifting one leg
Standing and turning
Dancing

Foreshortening

The technique of drawing part of a subject smaller than it really is to make it appear to project towards or away from the viewer is called 'foreshortening'.

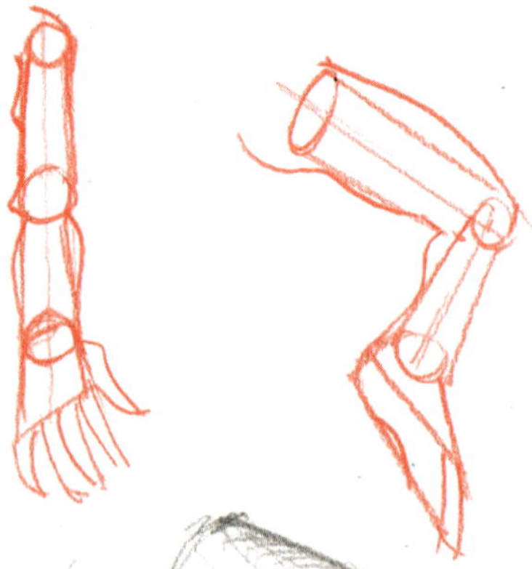

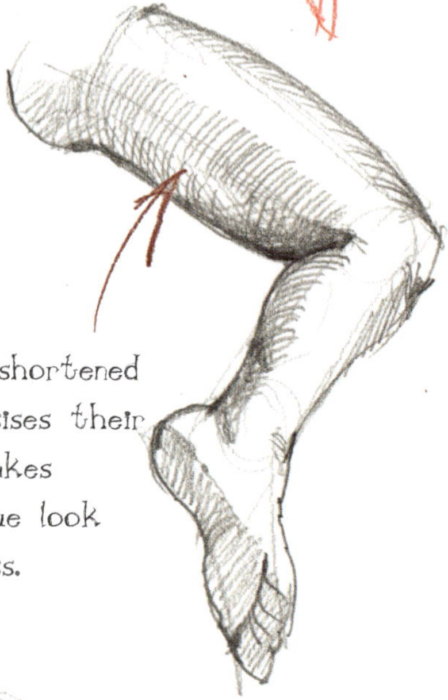

Shading foreshortened limbs emphasises their form and makes the technique look more seamless.

In this drawing of a reclining nude, the legs have been foreshortened. Shading along the length of the body helps to clarify the position of the limbs in relationship to the body as a whole.

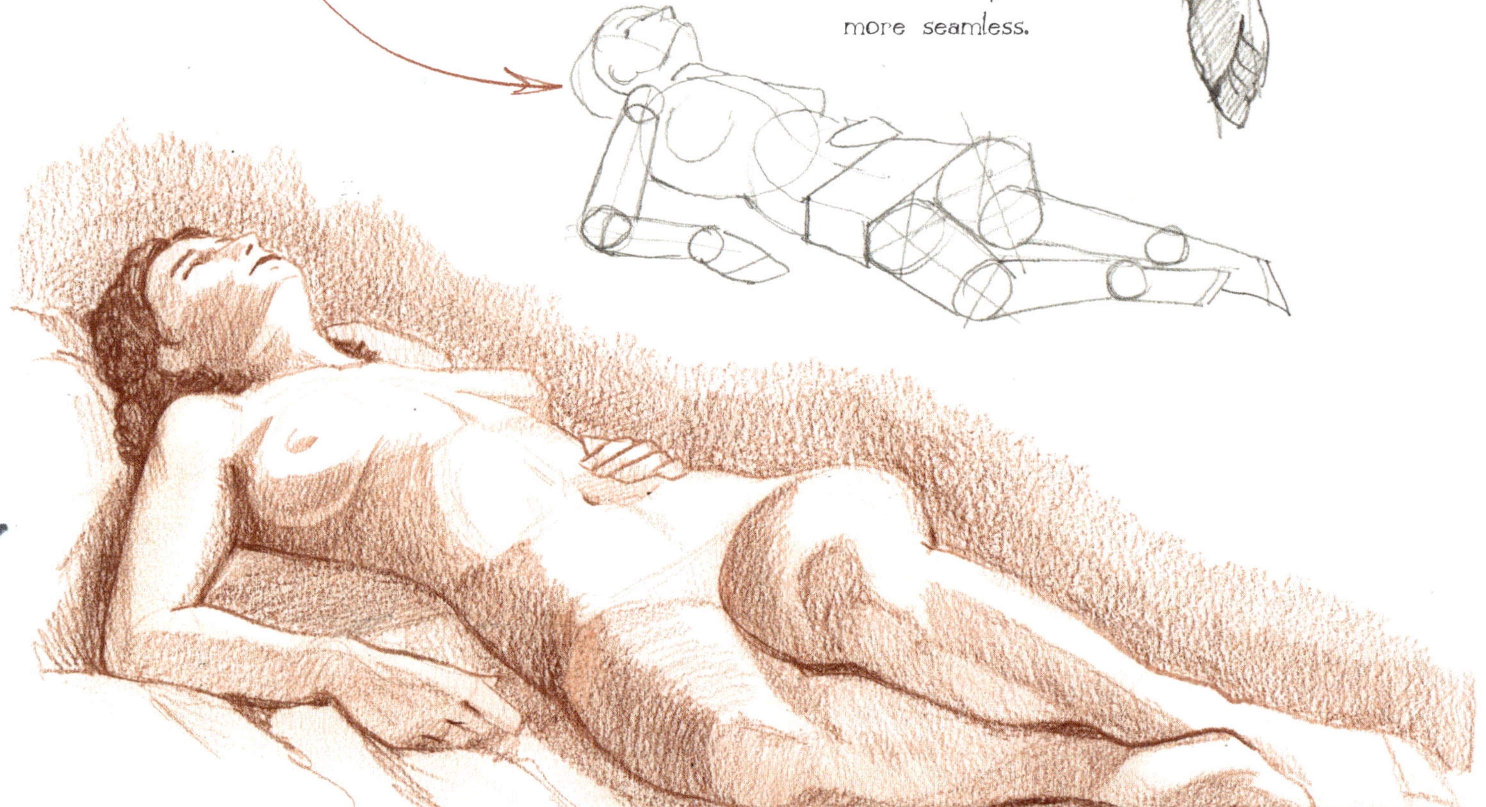

Use construction lines to help you correctly position the foreshortened parts of the body in relation to the rest. This creates a more convincing illusion of depth.

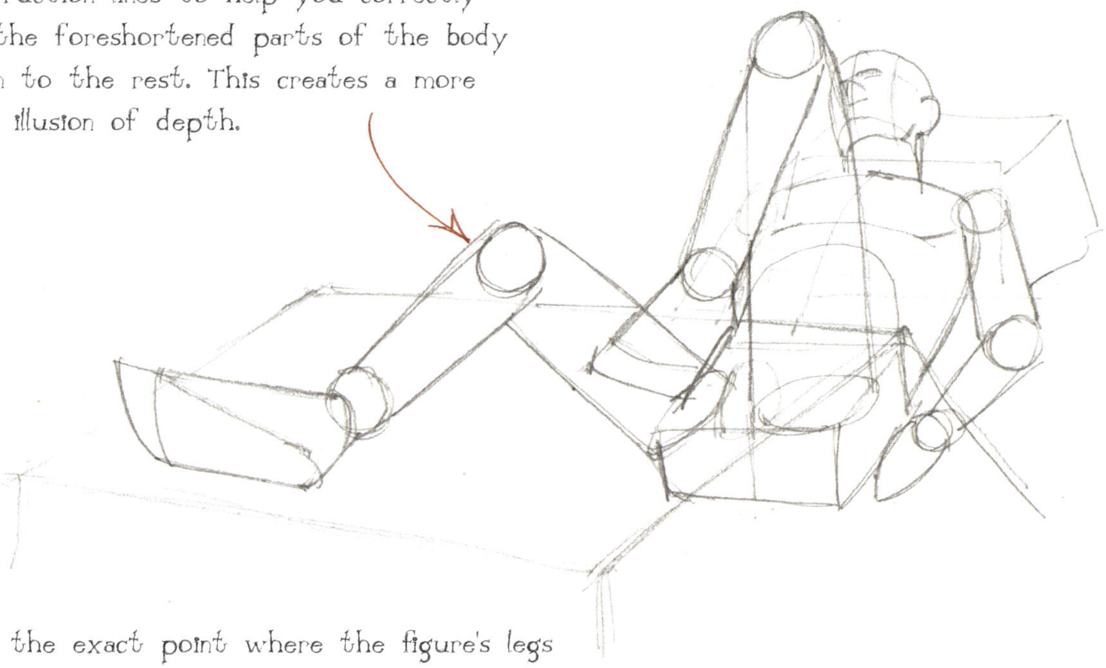

Although the exact point where the figure's legs join the body is hidden, it is crucial to get this relationship right in order to draw this pose correctly. The figure must be constructed as though it were visible in its entirety in order to relate the elevated angle of the legs to the body.

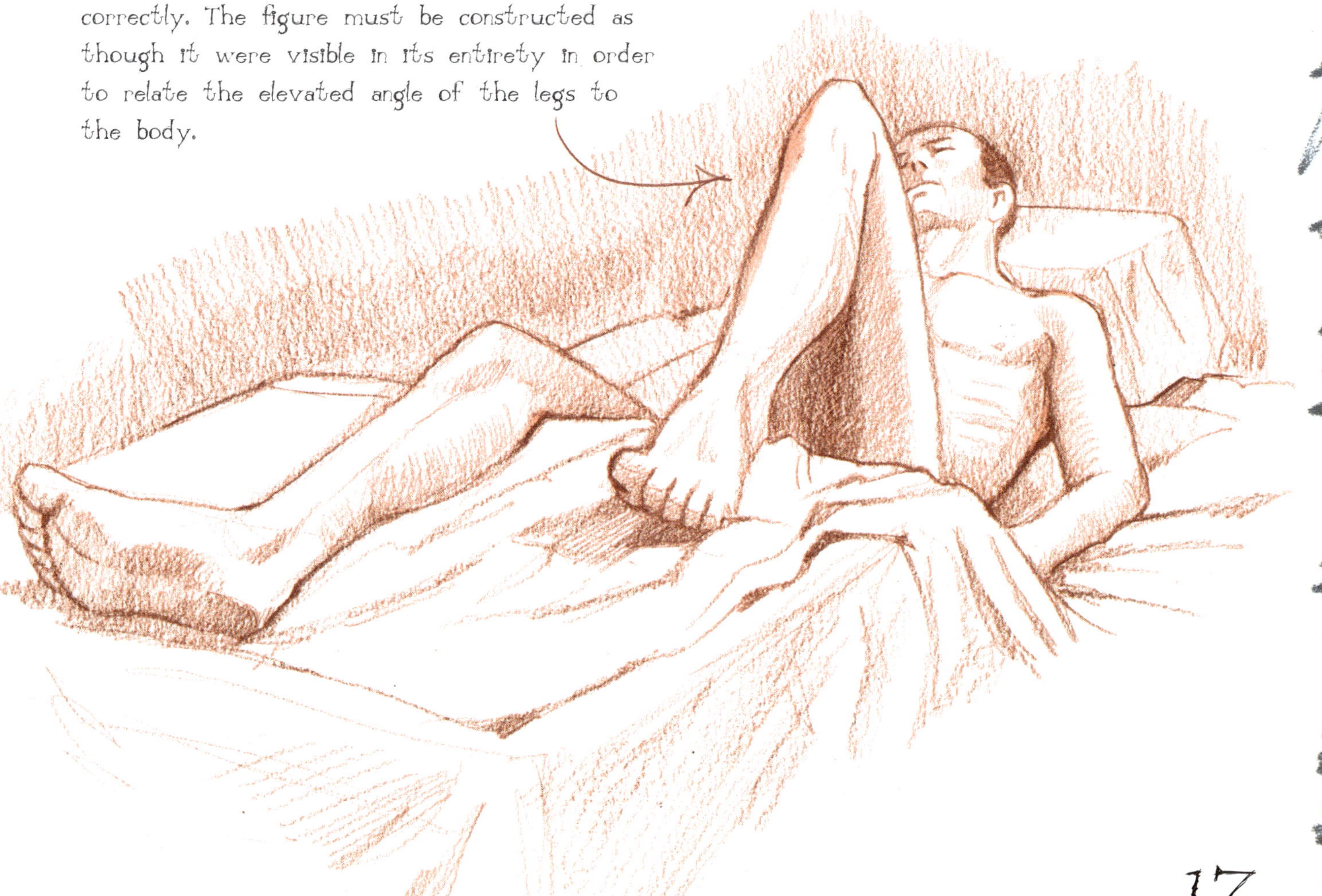

Light & shade

There are several aspects of light that must be considered in any drawing of a nude figure. The direction of the light source is crucial but be aware, too, of the quality of light and the shadows it creates.

The use of hatching in ink line drawings emphasises the direction of the light source, and the shadows it casts over the figure.

Coloured pencils can be used to convey warm or cold light hues as they hit your subject.

Coloured pastels are particularly good for conveying softer, more muted types of light.

Pencils can emphasise the way light can make skin glow, and gives definition to the shape of the body.

Geometrising

Rendering the complex form of the human body in simple geometric shapes, such as spheres, cubes and pyramids, is called geometrising. It's a useful way of reducing the human figure to its essence and thereby making it easier to draw.

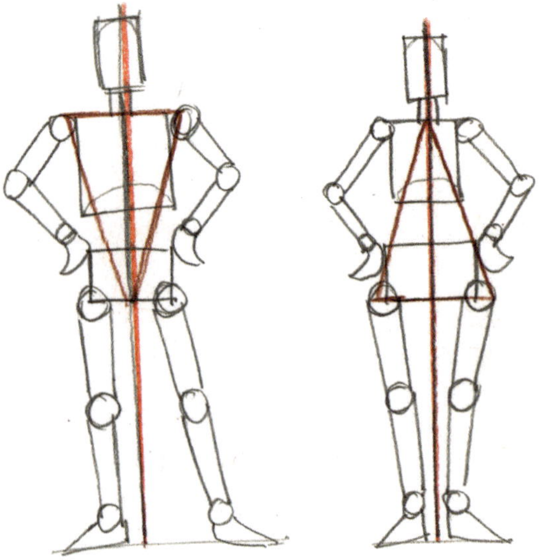

Using an inverted triangle for the male torso and an upright triangle for the female torso is an effective way of establishing the different body structure of men and women.

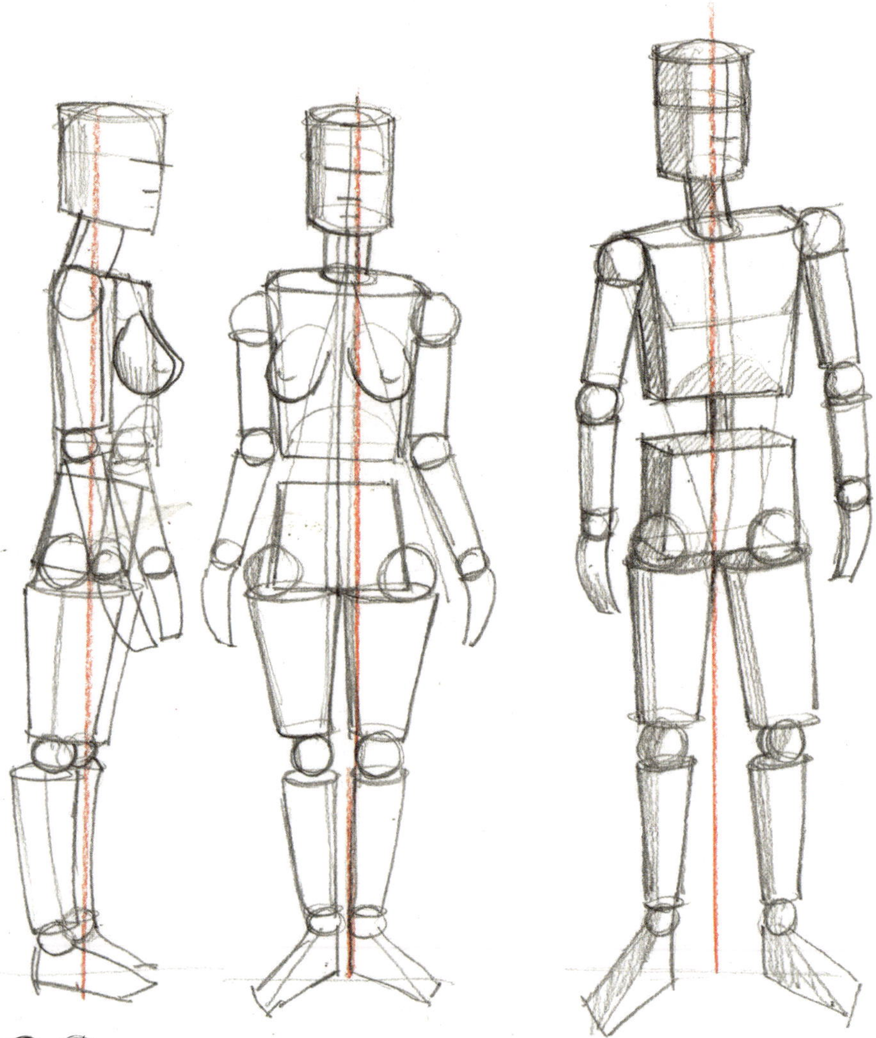

Use simple cylinder, sphere and cube shapes to practise drawing human figures in different positions, and see how it affects their posture.

Start with a rectangle for the head and a curved line for the spine. Add rectangles for the torso and hips. Then sketch in the arms and legs using cylinder shapes with circles for the joints. Add simple shapes for the hands and feet.

Sitting, cross-legged

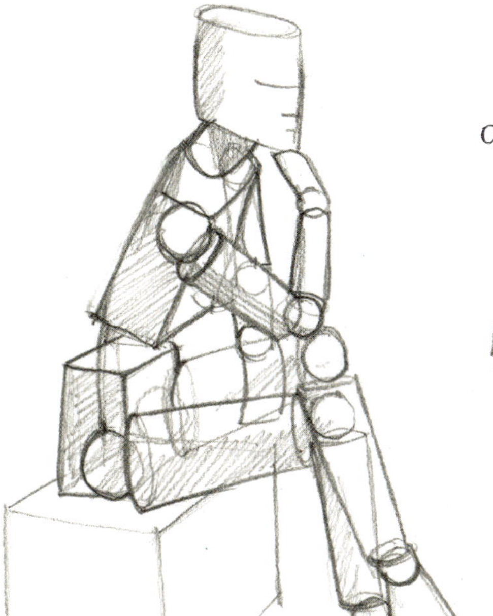

Cowering

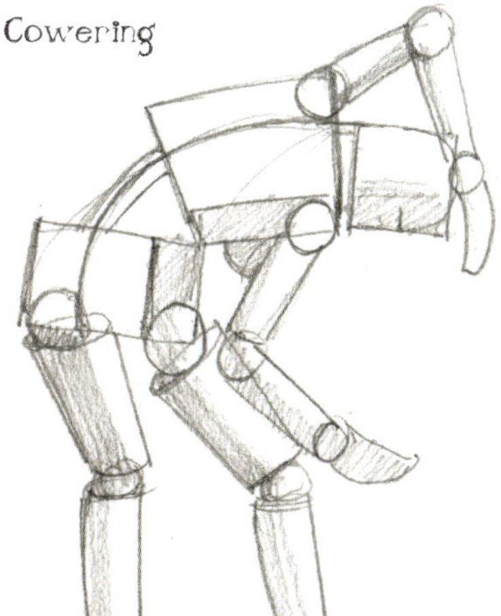

Defensive

Pastel pencil sketch

The softness and texture of a pastel pencil makes it perfect for capturing skin tones. It is an ideal drawing material for nude figure studies.

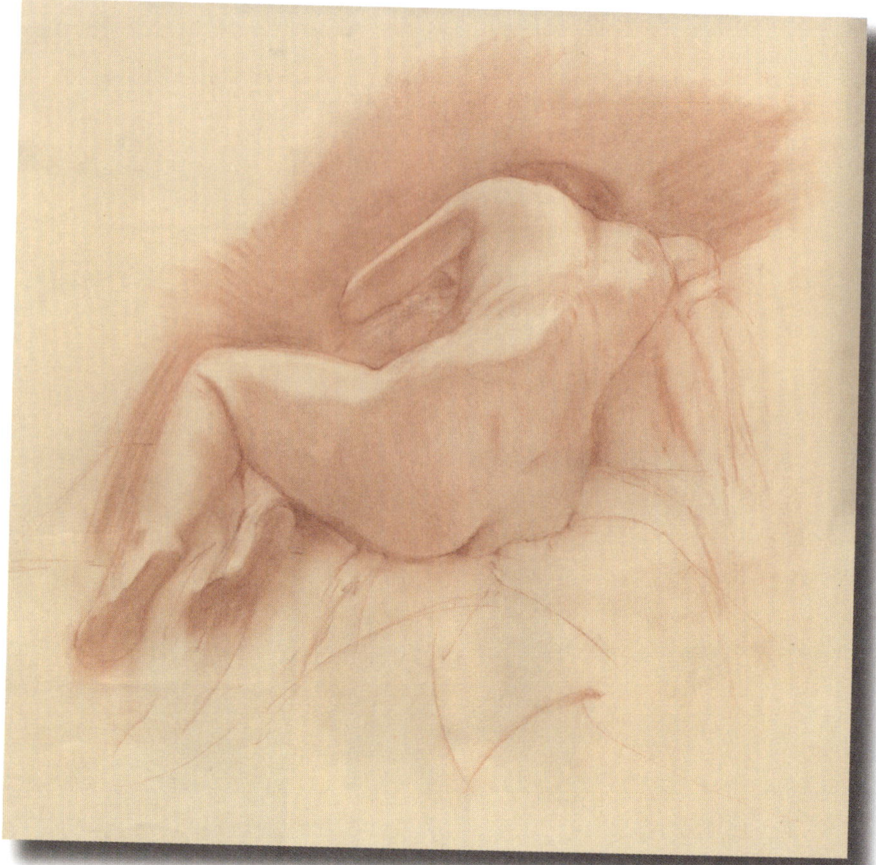

This is an example of a pastel sketch showing a bold use of light and tone. This drawing was created in an hour.

If you cannot practise by attending a life drawing class, then use photographic reference instead.

Start with a sketchy gestural drawing of the figure. Use simple shapes to capture the position and posture.

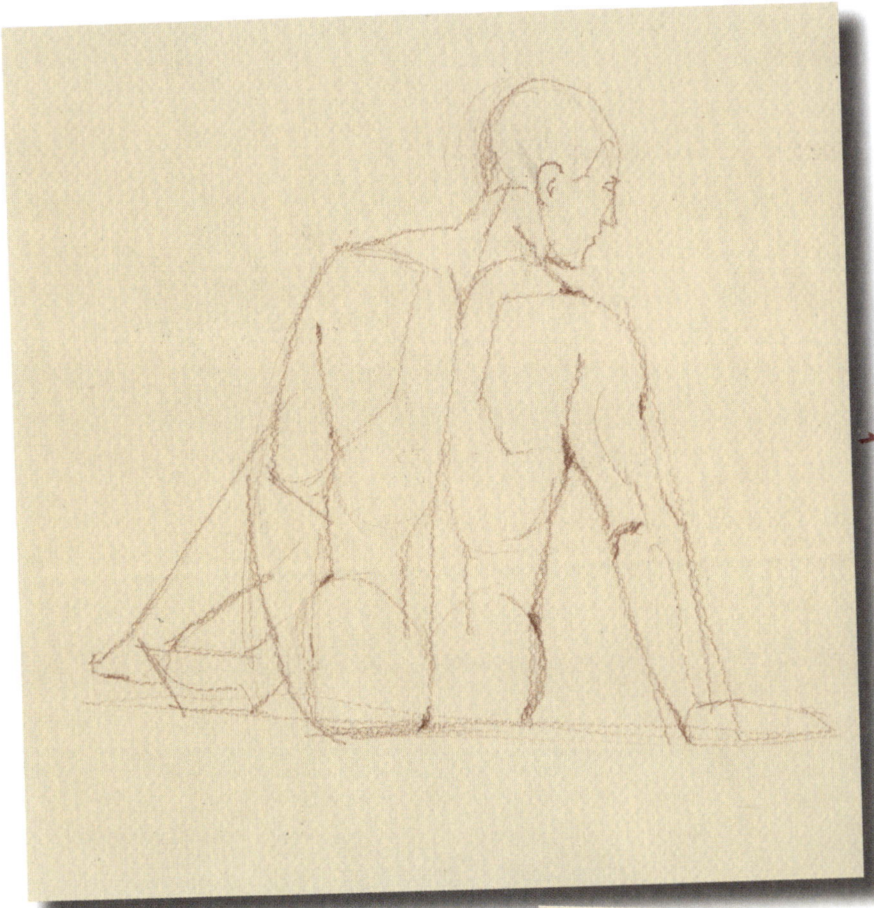

Define the outline of the figure and erase any excess lines. Now think about the anatomy and add lines to define the position of the muscles. Draw in the hair and the facial features.

Add shading to define the hair and stubble, and to show which parts of the body are in shadow.

Erase any unwanted construction lines.

Charcoal drawing

The slightly messy nature of charcoal makes it a very lively material for capturing the dynamic quality of the human figure.

These two charcoal drawings were both five-minute sketches. They show that you can quickly get great results using charcoal.

The charcoal drawing below was a quick sketch, using this photograph as a reference.

Charcoal is ideal for conveying the softness of skin and the curves of the human body, because it can be smudged and blended to give the drawing a soft, flowing texture.

Pen & wash technique

This technique combines the precision and sharpness of an ink line with the warm softness and tone created by diluted watercolour washes.

Experiment with different watercolour washes to find tones that suit your subject.

Using a photographic reference allows you to squeeze in extra practice with any technique. Start by pencilling in a basic outline of the figure.

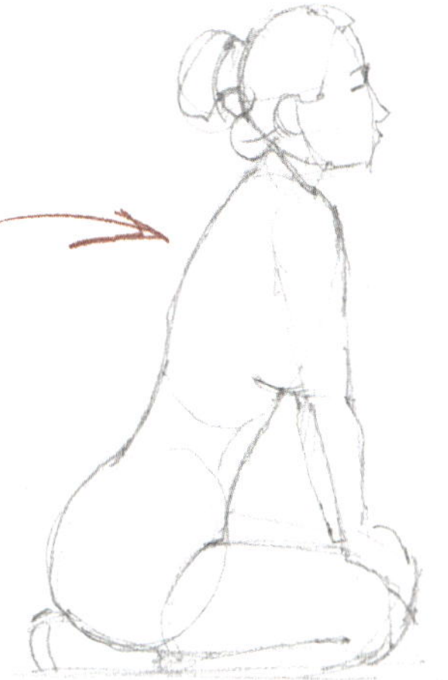

Then carefully ink in the outline. Draw in the facial features and the hair and finish off all details.

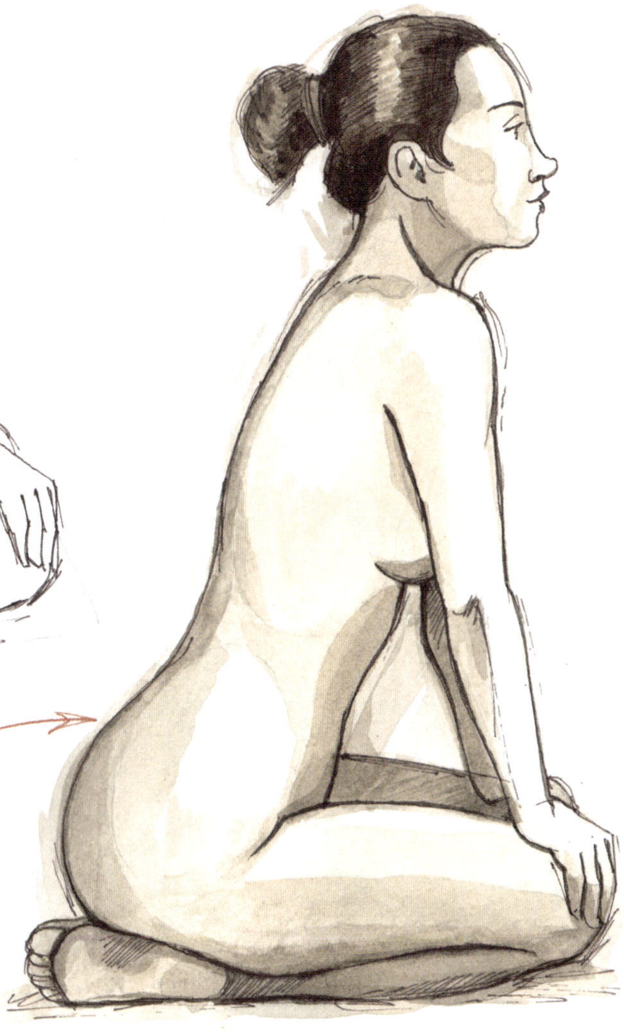

Now use watercolour washes to add the skin and hair tone and to define the intensity and colour of the light hitting your subject.

Shading techniques

To add realistic shading to a nude figure, you first need to take into account the direction of the light source. Then consider the subject's pose and the shape of their body and musculature.

Negative space

The negative space around your subject can quickly alert you to any problem areas in the drawing.

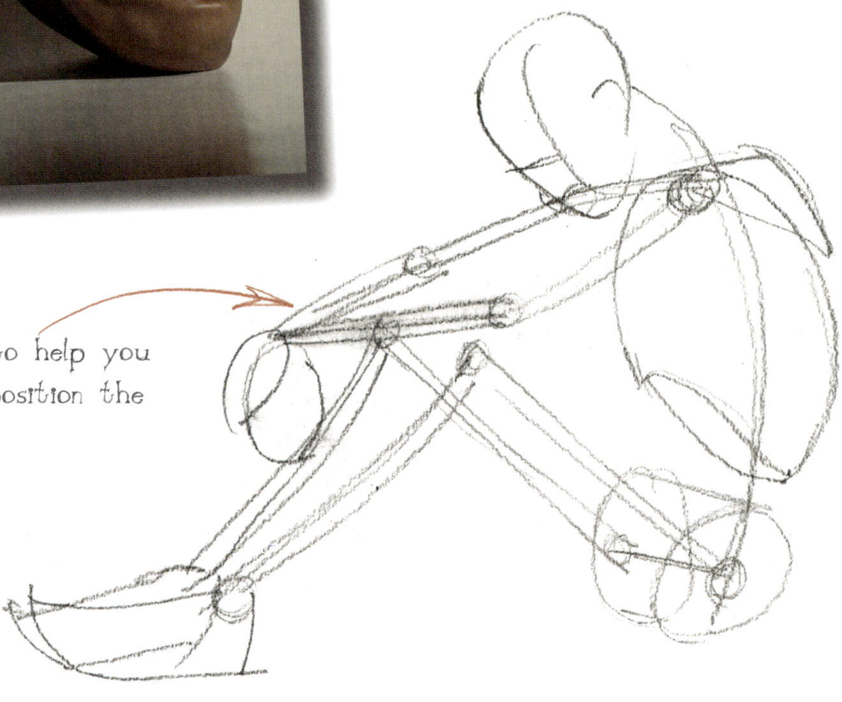

Use an artist's mannequin to help you correctly proportion and position the pose you're drawing.

Start drawing in the body shape. Use the body's visible 'landmarks' – those parts of the underlying bone structure that create the overall shape.

Light source

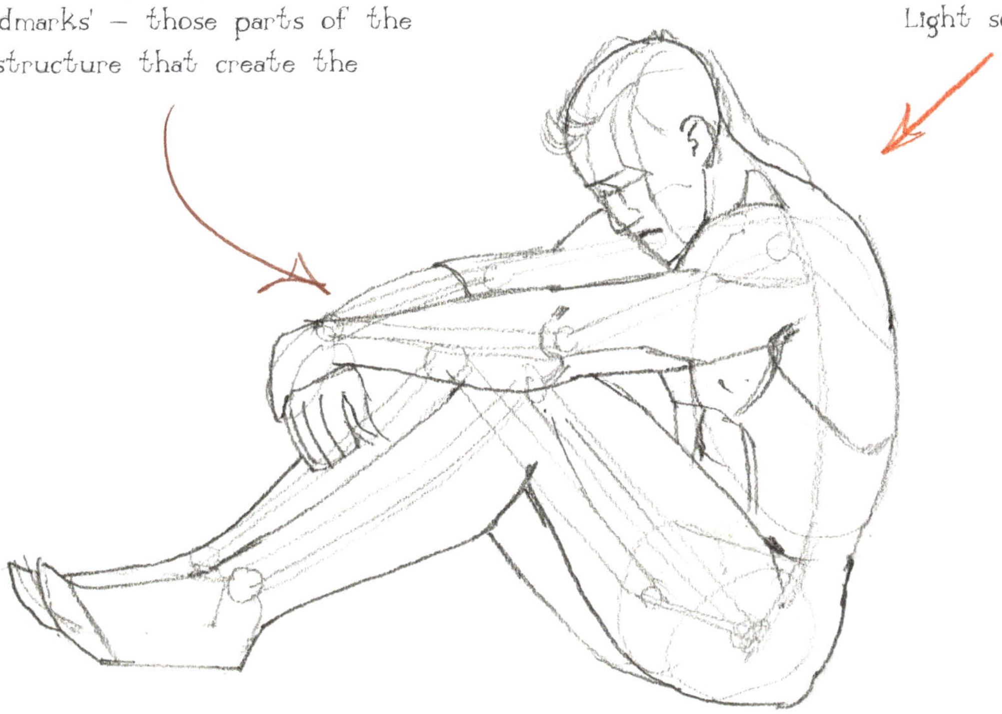

As the light source comes from the right-hand side, most of the shading and shadows are on the left-hand side of the subject. Use a wide tonal range, with the darkest in areas where light does not reach. Add shadows under the seated figure to 'ground' it, and shadows cast on the wall.

Use a putty rubber to create highlights.

Erase any unwanted construction lines.

Pastel on pastel

This pastel drawing has been done on pastel paper. Pastel paper comes in a range of colours which can be used as an integral part of a drawing. In this example, the paper colour has been used to create the lightest tones.

Use A Mirror

Try looking at your drawing in a mirror. Seeing it in reverse often helps you to spot mistakes.

Pastel papers are soft and easily marked with an eraser. First make an accurate pencil drawing on white paper. Scribble over the back of the drawing to transfer it onto a coloured pastel sheet. Now draw over the lines using a pastel crayon.

Add mid-tones to the figure using the same pastel crayon. Areas left untouched will become the lightest tones. Now use a darker crayon to add a stronger, contrasting background tone.

As before, start by making an accurate pencil drawing on white paper and transferring it onto a coloured pastel sheet. Draw over the lines using a pastel crayon.

This drawing is more complex and has a much greater tonal range. It took about 90 minutes to complete.

Glossary

Construction lines Guidelines used in the early stages of a drawing; they may be erased later.

Cross-hatching The use of criss-crossed lines to indicate dense shade in a drawing.

Hatching The use of parallel lines to indicate light shade in a drawing.

Negative space The empty space between the parts of a drawing, often an important part of the composition.

Perspective A method of drawing in which near objects are shown larger than faraway objects to give an impression of depth.

Index